A Conversation with Mayor
Marion Barry

A Conversation with Mayor

Marion Barry

Held on April 10, 1979
at the American Enterprise Institute for Public Policy Research
Washington, D.C.

ISBN 0–8447–3347–4

Library of Congress Catalog Card No. 79-89832

AEI Studies 244

Printed in the United States of America

Introduction

Marion Barry, the mayor of Washington, D.C., was born on March 6, 1936, in Itta Bena, Mississippi, and grew up in Memphis, Tennessee, where he received his early education in the public schools. He earned a bachelor's degree from LeMoyne College, a degree in chemistry from Fisk University, and later began his doctoral studies at the University of Tennessee.

Feeling the press of increasing involvement in the massive voter registration drives and antidiscrimination movement in the South, Marion Barry interrupted his doctoral program to devote his talents fully to the organization and direction of the Student Non-Violent Coordinating Committee (SNCC). He became its first national chairman in 1960. On becoming director of the Washington SNCC office in 1965, Mr. Barry worked in cooperation with other activists, and in 1966 organized a successful bus boycott against a fare increase and created the Free D.C. Movement.

In 1967 Mr. Barry co-founded Pride, Incorporated, a pilot self-help job-training program. Continuing his public life in the political arena, Mr. Barry was elected to the School Board in 1971; he was immediately elected its president and served in that capacity for about two and a half years. During this time, he unified the divided and troubled board.

In 1974 Mr. Barry was elected City Council member-at-large and was reelected by 73 percent of the vote in 1976. In addition to serving as chairman of the Committee of Finance and Revenue, Mr. Barry's accomplishments as councilman include legislation for tax relief and tax credits for elderly, blind, and disabled homeowners and renters; increased funding for public education at the grade school, high school, and college levels; and, with others, the creation of the Office of Aging and sponsorship of the Minority Contracting Act of 1976.

On January 21, 1978, Mr. Barry announced his candidacy for mayor, urging concerned citizens to take a stand for a competent

1

government. In ensuing months, he received endorsements from diverse groups, including labor unions, civic associations, the *Washington Post*, Americans for Democratic Action, an informal coalition of artists, youth groups, gay rights activists, feminist organizations, and others. With 34.6 percent of the Democratic electorate casting their votes for him in the primary election in September, Mr. Barry emerged as the unifying force in the Democratic party.

On November 7, Mr. Barry won the general election in a race with the Republican candidate, Arthur Fletcher. He was sworn in by Chief Justice Thurgood Marshall on January 2, 1979, as the second elected mayor of the District of Columbia. He pledged that his administration will be a "partnership with the people."

ROBERT L. WOODSON
Resident Fellow
American Enterprise Institute

A Conversation with
Mayor Marion Barry

This is a great opportunity to share—particularly with those who are not from this area—some of the ideas and visions and attitudes I have about the District of Columbia government.

Too often, people who visit or even work in Washington see the District of Columbia as a city of monuments: the Washington Monument, the Capitol, the White House, the Smithsonian. But it is a city of people—more than 700,000 of them. We are not only a city, but also a county and state, in terms of our legislative function and our taxing and program authorities. We have some of the same problems that other cities, counties, and states have, and we have the additional problem of being the only group of citizens in the United States of America who do not have a vote in the Congress.

We are larger than seven states. We pay over $1.4 billion a year in federal income taxes but receive only about $450 million back. We have had more casualties in wars than eleven states in the history of this country, yet we do not have a vote in the Congress.

Other states and cities and counties at least have representation, but we do not vote for a senator of any kind. It has been suggested that we vote with Maryland, but I do not like that idea. Marylanders do not want Baltimore and Washington to team up to elect a new kind of senator, or two senators, and we do not want it either. We ought to have our own two senators and our fair share of congressional representatives. Walter Fauntroy, the congressman from the District, has a voice in the Congress, but no vote.

Increasingly, the federal government is getting into our business—the individual's business, as well as states' and cities' and counties' business. It is an added disadvantage that we do not have anyone to state our case in the Senate or on the floor of the House.

Washington, D.C., is similar to most urban cities in the Northeast.

3

It is an old city with a number of decaying neighborhoods, and it has more than its share of the indexes of poverty. For instance, more than 18 percent of the people in the District of Columbia are over sixty years of age, compared with 9 or 10 percent in Maryland and Virginia, which is an added burden. More than 200,000 of our people are receiving some type of aid, such as social security benefits, Medicaid or Medicare, Aid to Families with Dependent Children, or a number of other welfare payments. We have to carry more than our fair share of the region's poverty, in that sense.

We are glad to do that, but it costs money and we are limited, to some extent, because the federal government owns more than 50 percent of the land. There is supposed to be a federal payment to the city in lieu of taxes, but that comes to only 19 percent of our total budget. To give a comparison, in the city of Gary, Indiana, U.S. Steel owns more than 50 percent of the land, and it pays about 51 percent of the total tax revenues, which shows how unbalanced our federal payment is. We believe that it ought to be at least 50 percent of our locally raised revenues. Therefore, we are carrying the federal government; it is not carrying us.

Can you imagine the value of the land around the White House? If we could use that land commercially and collect corporate taxes and income taxes and other kinds of taxes from it, we would not be so limited.

We are limited in other ways as well. For example, if we had anticipated that, in the fall of 1979 or the spring of 1980, we would need to purchase two more ambulances because we expected the number of emergency trauma cases to increase, the process would have had to start in the spring of 1978. At that time the Department of Human Resources or the Fire Department would have put into its budget the cost of two ambulances, say, $20,000, and ten drivers. That would have gone to the Council in September of 1978. The Council would have taken fifty days to consider the District budget with those two ambulances in it; it would have gone back to the mayor in December of 1978, and the mayor would have signed it. The total D.C. budget would then have gone to the President of the United States—this year it went on January 16, because I made sure we got it there early; ordinarily it would have gone in March because of delays.

From the President it would have gone to the Congress, both the House and the Senate, on February 1. And then it would have gone to the Appropriations Committee of the House, the Appropriations Committee of the Senate, then to the subcommittee on the District of Columbia, headed by Senator Leahy in the Senate and Congressman Wilson in the House. They would have held hearings in the spring of

4

1979, as they are doing now, and sometime in June or July the sub-committees would mark up our D.C. budget with our two ambulances in it, would send it back to the congressional committees, back to the full Congress, then to the President, and maybe our 1980 budget would be approved by October 1 of 1979. Only then could we purchase the two ambulances.

I give that example to show how difficult it is to budget and to operate in the District. We have to start almost eighteen months before trying to purchase something. Most cities and most counties and states have reprogramming authority whereby they could have appropriated the money for those two ambulances in a week or ten days—or at most two months.

In addition to social problems, we have budgetary constraints, since our budget is approved by the Congress of the United States and the president. And yet more than 80 percent of all the money that is raised in the District comes out of the pockets of those who live, work, and do business in this town.

We were confronted, on January 2, with a city government that was rather inefficiently run and with rather ineffective programs. In fact, some people here and around the country probably considered the District government the laughingstock of the nation. I have met people at conventions who were ashamed to admit they were from the District. They would say they were from Maryland or somewhere else.

We have tried from the beginning to demonstrate that this government could be managed. I have insisted that public servants be public servants and deliver services to people, including answering the telephone courteously. We have told our employees that courtesy is important.

In Washington, as in most other cities, there are probably six or seven major areas of great concern, and one is economic development. In the Northeast particularly, most cities are suffering from an out-migration of people and businesses. Since 1968 more than 1,500 businesses have left the District of Columbia in the retail goods and services sector alone. We therefore have to work very hard to create a climate that will attract businesses into the District of Columbia and keep those that are here. But economic development has to be weighed against neighborhood movements and citizen participation. A number of people in neighborhoods such as Dupont Circle and Georgetown, for instance, say there are enough businesses there. They do not want their neighborhoods commercialized any more than they are.

The other question is one of jobs. In the District of Columbia more than 60 percent of all the black young people between the ages of eighteen and twenty-five are out of work, and more than 20 percent of

5

all our citizens are out of work. Unemployment is a very serious problem.

We are almost a company town in the sense that the federal bureaucracy dominates what happens here, and it is very difficult to create semiskilled and unskilled jobs. Most jobs in the District are white-collar, and though some are blue-collar, they usually require skills.

We have to figure out how to create unskilled jobs. I have set a goal of 30,000 jobs this summer in the public sector. By taking CETA[1] money and supplementing it with D.C. funds of about $12 million, I hope to make 30,000 jobs, compared with 14,000 jobs last summer.

Another job-related problem in the District is a federal law that prohibits children from working in public sector jobs if their parents make above a certain amount of money. The purpose of this law is to keep people who do not need the work or the money from ripping off the system. But it works against the needs of the city, because about 47 percent of all the households in the District are single-parent households and probably about 80–85 percent of those households have female heads. If they are making $8,000 or more, their children cannot work. We have tried to overcome that difficulty with our local funding.

Jobs are a very serious problem, not only locally but nationally. It has to be tackled by the national government. That is why I am dismayed that the present administration is proposing to reduce the number of CETA jobs in 1980. Only at the national level can we get the kind of help that we need. I believe the government is an employer of last resort, and I fought hard for the original Humphrey-Hawkins Bill—not the final compromise, though I understand why it was necessary.

In a program the size of CETA—almost $6 billion, I think—there are bound to be some people who take advantage of it. And it bothers me a great deal that this gives other people an excuse to cut the program down or cut it out. I think we need more, not less, money for jobs.

The same is true with housing. In the District of Columbia more than 150,000 people are considered displaceable: either they rent from someone who can put them out in 120 days by merely issuing a writ of restitution taking back the property, or they pay more than 35 percent of their income in rent. More than 30,000 families are in that category, which means that if rents go up those families cannot afford to stay where they are. Since 1968, more than 75,000 people have been displaced in this city, a large portion of them through urban renewal, sometimes called "blight removal."

---

[1]Comprehensive Employment and Training Act.

We have said that housing is a national problem, and we have urged the national administration to spend more money on housing. Again, in 1980 we are going to get less money for housing, not more.

Section 8 has been a good program, but it has been too little, too late. In fact, there is now a move away from Section 8, which is a scattered site subsidy program, back into a public housing program. Over a thirty-year period, units will cost about $120,000, with amortization and interest, and it is said to be easier to build public housing at $40,000 a unit and be finished with it, as opposed to the private-public sector partnership.

We have tried to establish a tone by saying that housing owned by the D.C. government ought to set an example. About a month ago we announced a major program to take the boards off of 733 units of housing—that is 98 percent of all the houses that are owned by the D.C. government. Included are 184 public housing units that we are going to renovate and put people in. There are more than 11,900 public housing units in the District and over 6,000 families waiting to get them. Obviously, the need is there. It takes an average of four and a half years for a family to get into our most heavily subsidized housing, which is called "public housing."

We are trying to get the private sector to do more, but because of rent control and other kinds of control, private builders say that they are not going to build. I think we have had only one new, nonsubsidized housing unit built since 1976 in the District of Columbia. But more than 10,000 units are eligible for condominium conversion in 1978 compared with 1,500 in 1977. Many of those conversions are in the area of Dupont Circle and Ward Three.

I brought in one of the most dynamic, brilliant, bright, and compassionate housing directors in the country, Bob Moore. He did a great job in Houston for about three years, heading their Public Housing Authority. I also brought in a very able city administrator from Berkeley, Elijah Rogers. Together we are working on housing, trying to do all we can with what we have, but it is not enough. We cannot solve this problem without national help and support.

I gave the whole question of health a very high priority in this administration. This city has the highest infant mortality rate, of any major American city, 27.3 per 1,000. The national average is about 14 deaths per 1,000. It is an index of the health of the community. Along with infant mortality, we have the highest tuberculosis rate, the highest cancer rate, particularly among black males, the highest venereal disease rate. I have taken on health as a major issue because if our community is not physically and mentally healthy, it cannot be spiritually, economically, culturally, and politically healthy.

These are some of the things that I have been trying to do in this administration. If we solve a problem in the District of Columbia, the solution can be duplicated around the country, because the problems in New York are not much different from those of Washington, Cleveland, or Chicago.

In the Southwest problems are a little different because cities such as Houston and Dallas have expansion room. They are newer cities and they are not asking for as much federal help as we are in the East because they are able to expand physically and industrially. Bob Moore told me when he came from Houston that it was very difficult to get the mayor of Houston to apply for federal grants because there was enough money down there. That is unusual, and when he comes here for the Conference of Mayors I'm going to find out if I can import some of it.

I am very proud of the government in the District of Columbia. I am proud that the people chose me to be the mayor. I love the District, I love the people here, I love a lot of things that are going on here, including our public schools. I do not like everything in them, and sometimes I do not like the way our School Board acts, but that is a continuing debate between school boards and mayors all over the country.

I have said to our School Board—and I was on it for two and a half years—that it cannot be an island unto itself. It cannot use more than $250 million of the taxpayers' money and not be asked some questions about what it is doing with the money. When teachers go on strike, the School Board must be concerned that 116,000 young people are being shortchanged educationally. I stepped into the strike here, and the parents and the teachers seem to be happy I did; some members of the board are not happy, but I am not running a popularity contest, so I don't worry about that, as long as the schools are open.

Being the mayor of the District of Columbia brings added responsibilities. Not only are we a local city, but we are also the nation's capital. The Conference of Mayors and the League of Cities are both located in Washington, and they ask me almost every other day to testify somewhere on the Hill. I cannot always do that. There are 176 black mayors in America, and I am the mayor of the third largest of the cities that have them. I try to help out the other black mayors when they call me about a question. I can pick up the telephone and get an answer, whereas many of them do not have plane fare to come here themselves. I think that is another role I have to play. I am trying to devote all of my energies to the District, but, on the other hand, I feel that I have to try to represent my brother and sister mayors around the country.

8

Questions and Answers

JACK LIMPERT, editor of *Washingtonian Magazine:* Fifteen years ago, when you first came here, D.C. had a special relationship with the White House. It was considered an example and a laboratory. Do you feel that is much less the case now?

MAYOR BARRY: I think we probably have a better relationship this year with the White House than we had fourteen or fifteen years ago when I first came to the District. I have met with the President specifically on D.C. concerns, and there are four or five people in the White House who now look after D.C. problems.

I was asked after January whether I would recommend that there be one person in the administration to handle D.C. affairs as there was fourteen or fifteen years ago, and I said no. I think that would be a mistake. It puts too much responsibility on one person, and it bottles things up in one person.

HOBART TAYLOR, attorney: I think you have earned the admiration of everybody around here for the energy and for the analytical powers that you have brought to the problems of the District since you have taken office.

You mentioned the problem of condominium conversions and that no rental units are being built in the District. You recognize the importance of rent control, but at the same time you have the problem of what would happen if all rent controls went off. Nobody can move because no one knows what the costs are going to be in a year or two, and they have to build at today's costs. They don't know what utility bills are going to be, or anything else.

Do you have any approach that will enable capital to flow into the District under the same, or approximately similar, conditions as in other places?

MAYOR BARRY: It is a tough problem. Rent control was on the books when I became a Council member, and, politically, it is difficult for any elected official in this city to be against rent control in some form or fashion.

We are trying to develop more housing units. That is tough without subsidy, because a one-bedroom unit built at today's costs would probably end up having to be rented for about $400 or a little more per month.

We are working on an overall condominium conversion program. I am opposed to a blanket moratorium on condominium conversions.

9

On the other hand, I am sensitive to the plight of those who have lived in these units for ten or fifteen years. Some of them are elderly—senior citizens who do not want to buy or cannot afford to. We are trying to get a modified condominium conversion law, but the problem is that potential investors are very nervous about whatever we do. If we took all the controls off condominium conversion, they would be nervous because they know that if we take them off on April 10, we can put them back on May 10. The Council has that authority, and the mayor can sign the act.

I don't have a real solution, except that we have started with a private-public partnership to take the boards off D.C.-owned houses. This is going to cost $35 million; we are taking $10 million of our public money and $25 million from savings and loans and from commercial banks to put this package together. That's a start, and we can go forward from there.

We have had a problem with progress payments for people who do work for the D.C. government. We have bankrupted some people; we now deposit our money for those progress payments in the bank, and people can draw it out on progress.

We are trying to put together a $6 million program with the Economic Development Administration. It will provide some up-front money for developers to take the risk out of a major building program on 14th Street. We are also trying to encourage development of middle-income townhouses in the Southeast section of Washington. Bob Moore is meeting with the bankers about mortgages, and I think the commercial bank and savings and loans are beginning to get some confidence in this administration and will help out.

If we can expand our housing stock, which will be tough, there is a possibility of bringing some relief from rent control—maybe in terms of luxury units, of vacancy decontrol, or some other form of decontrol. But that will not restore confidence in the market until people have had two or three years to see that this city means business.

HERBERT STEIN, American Enterprise Institute: I remember the great enthusiasm that you generated in this area in 1967 when you organized Pride, which was a self-help movement. What has become of the self-help movement? All we hear now is the need for more appropriations from the federal government, more appropriations from the city government. Is there still a self-help movement here, and is it making progress?

MAYOR BARRY: Pride is still alive and well, and I still believe that communities have to help themselves. I don't think the government should do everything; it should not fund everything, it should not run everything. But we are finding that the problems are so deeply rooted that it requires a tremendous amount of money to do anything in terms of jobs and training and education. At Pride, it probably costs between $6,000 and $7,000 a year to train somebody. The CETA Program, Title II, is supposed to encourage community groups to help themselves and to use CETA employees to offset some of the cost. But in an area such as housing, no matter how strongly we feel about self-help, we cannot build housing without some money.

This summer we are going to put a large number of young people to work in our public housing projects to do landscaping, minor carpentry, electrical repair, and window glazing. But that is just a drop in the bucket, compared with what needs to be done. It is going to cost money.

DR. STEIN: The record of the CETA program as a way of preparing people for employment in the private sector is, at least on a national scale, pretty miserable. Something seems to be missing other than the billions of dollars that have been spent. We do not seem to know how to operate those programs so as to turn out qualified and ambitious workers.

MAYOR BARRY: I think there are several things missing. The reason that we cannot get private sector employment in the District is not necessarily the fault of the CETA workers; it is the fault of the private employers who will not employ people. For example, hotels and restaurants in this city for whatever reason, would rather employ foreigners. People who cannot even speak English are hired as waiters.

Maybe the problem is attitudinal. Employers figure that because a person is a CETA trainee he might not bring to the job the skills or the attitudes that any other worker would bring. But I do not think that is the case. We have some CETA workers in the District government who are at the GS-3 and GS-4 levels, but on the basis of their academic record and experience they ought to be able to get government service jobs at the GS-9 and GS-10 levels. We found a number of lawyers working at CETA who had passed the bar, but they just could not get any other work.

I don't know the answer. When I met with Secretary of Labor Marshall about a month ago, I suggested that we get some statistical information or attitudinal information as to why, around the country, cities are having a problem placing CETA workers in private employment.

Many cities and counties and states, including the District before I got here, used the CETA program as a substitute. Because their local tax dollars were shrinking and they were facing an attrition of personnel, they would substitute a CETA position for a regular position with no intention of trying to train that worker or put him on the permanent payroll.

That is why there is now the requirement that a CETA employee can be kept on for only twelve months in the public service sector and eighteen months in the whole program. It is an attempt to force states and cities and counties to make preparation for hiring CETA workers in permanent positions. I am getting ready to sign a mayor's order this week which instructs all our departments of government to give CETA workers first shot at any vacancy that occurs, if they are qualified. We have more than 2,200 CETA workers in the city, and often they are not notified of vacancies. That is one way that I'm going to try to get them jobs in the public sector. We also have Title VII, which is a private initiative program. We are establishing a private initiative council which I hope will get the business community more involved in hiring CETA workers.

By and large, the majority of the participants in the CETA program have wanted to learn and want to work, and the prime sponsors have run a fairly good program under the circumstances. It has been abused in some places, but, again, I do not think we ought to use the abuses as excuses for not funding, at a good level, public service employment. I believe that the federal government ought to be the employer of last resort, either through grants or through its own employment.

DR. STEIN: I would agree with you, but at what rate of pay?

MAYOR BARRY: I think it has to be at the minimum wage and go up from there. Some people say there ought to be different wages for public service employees who do the same kind of work. I disagree. If a Pride trainee has learned how to be a keypunch operator just as well as a person who is working for the government at the GS-4 level, why shouldn't we pay the same rate for the same amount of work?

There are also some people who say there ought to be a youth wage that is different from what an adult makes. I am sympathetic to that point of view, but I believe employers would hire young people and pay them less as a way of cutting costs. And I do not think that ought to happen.

Public service jobs have a stigma, but they ought not to be regarded as dead-end jobs that nobody else wants to do. When Lockheed gets a guarantee of a loan, it is subsidy, but when an AFDC[2]

---

[2]Aid to Families with Dependent Children.

mother gets a check, it is welfare. Maybe it ought to be the reverse—welfare for the rich and subsidy for the poor.

I think the CETA jobs are getting to be regarded as just something that is given away. It is thought that the program gives away all the government's money, and the people in it do not want to work anyway and are just getting government money free. We have to take away that stigma and make it an honorable way of getting into the work cycle.

The tragedy is that in Washington the CETA program costs an average of a little more than $7,200 a year per worker, with a maximum of $10,000 per person—$14,000 if the government subsidizes it. But it costs us $18,000 a year to keep somebody at Lorton, our local penitentiary. There is a direct correlation between jobs and unemployment and the reported crime rate and the criminal justice system.

BEN J. WATTENBERG, American Enterprise Institute: Jesse Jackson seems to be saying that motivation is the big problem in these areas. Do you agree with that?

MAYOR BARRY: Jesse Jackson and I agree that motivation is a major part of the problem. It is a question of helping ourselves, motivating ourselves, and getting parents involved in education. But even then it costs money to get these things done. And regardless of motivation, if a person finishes high school and cannot get a job, where is he?

As I said, 60 percent of District citizens between the ages of eighteen and twenty-five are out of work. We can encourage our young people, and get them to study at night and cut off the television from 7:00 to 9:00, and get their parents involved in their report cards. But no matter how motivated they are, the 6,000 seniors who are graduating this year cannot get a job in the District of Columbia.

WAYNE VALIS, American Enterprise Institute: Many political writers seem to feel that the D.C. Voting Rights Amendment is in trouble. What do you think?

MAYOR BARRY: In part it is having trouble because the political writers who predict this are prophets of doom and gloom. If they write it is in trouble then it gets in trouble. It is like the teacher who was told that certain children could not learn to read, and because she believed it they did not learn to read, while those who were described as able to learn did in fact learn.

Walter Fauntroy and D.C. City Council Chairman Arrington Dixon and I have just launched a new major effort, a voting rights service corporation. We have a five-year program to raise $5 million, and we are optimistic that we can attract a Board of Trustees of national stature—Republicans, Democrats, Independents, labor leaders, business leaders, and so forth. We have been in business about six weeks now, and already have raised $143,000 of our local share of $200,000 for this year's goal. We have an executive director, Tony Thompson, and we have the support of five states.

At first our friends in many states were so eager that they would introduce a resolution or a joint resolution before we were ready for it. Either we did not have the contacts or the people were, quite frankly, not politically the right ones to do it. We finally slowed them down and tried to coordinate efforts.

That has worked very effectively. But then our detractors and our enemies decided to try another tactic. In New Mexico they introduced a disapproval resolution before the question even came up and got it voted on in one day. New Mexico is therefore now in the loss column. But we are going to overcome that; we have six more years to get the amendment ratified.

The Equal Rights Amendment ought to be less controversial than D.C. voting rights, and that has not yet been ratified. It is very tough to get any constitutional amendment through. I guess the founding fathers made it tough so that it could not be done frivolously.

But I am optimistic that we are on track, and we are going to gather support from more states before the end of this year.

AUSTIN RANNEY, American Enterprise Institute: Mr. Mayor, many of us who are relatively new in town are very impressed with the Metro system. It is one of the best, maybe the best, I have ever seen in this country and maybe in the world. Do you think it has helped the downtown economy of Washington? Does it have potential that is not yet being realized? What kind of impact is it having or do you think it might have?

MAYOR BARRY: I agree with you that the Metro is the finest I have ever seen, and I have seen the ones in Tokyo, New York, San Francisco, Chicago, and a few other places. I believe in it. A hundred miles are being planned for the system; we have funding for sixty miles, and we are going to find funding for another forty miles, I guess, between the federal government and ourselves fairly soon.

It is just beginning to have an impact on the downtown economy. For a long time it did not extend into Maryland or Virginia, but now it extends to the east, south, and northeast, and we are beginning to see more and more people shopping downtown. The ridership has increased at night since the hours were extended to midnight, but I wish we could get more people to ride the Metro. It is heavily subsidized, but there is no public transportation that is not. The fares do not cover the costs. I think our fares are reasonable. The Metro is a great system—it is quiet, and it is the safest place to be. [Laughter.] I'm working now to get some murals painted at the entrances and elsewhere, to make the system even more attractive.

ARTHUR F. BURNS, American Enterprise Institute: If the federal government owns half the property in the District, it would seem reasonable that they should pay half the property taxes. But I understood you to say that you felt the federal payment should equal half the District's revenue. Could you explain why?

MAYOR BARRY: It is not only property taxes that we lose. Out of our $1.3 billion dollar budget, we receive about $196 million from residential and commercial property taxes; and we receive about $225 million from income taxes and about $120 million from sales taxes.

The land is only one factor. When there is a building on the land, people work in that building, and if they live in the District of Columbia then they pay income taxes, too. If there is a corporation in the building, it pays corporate taxes; if it is a profit-making enterprise it pays sales taxes on its purchases. Taking all these factors together, we lose about $500 million of potential revenue because the land is owned by the federal government.

Added to that is the problem that we cannot tax commuters who work here five days a week. Forty-one states have a commuter tax. For example, a commuter who lives in New Jersey and works in New York City pays the state of New York a reciprocal income tax, and pays the city of New York a commuter tax, then pays the Port Authority another tax to cross the bridge. We ought to have a commuter tax here. We are losing $200 million because we cannot tax the 266,000 people who only work here. We are working on a reciprocal tax, whereby those who live in Maryland or Virginia will not be double-taxed, but will deduct from their state taxes what they pay the District.

THE REVEREND CAMERON BYRD, Church of the Redeemer, Presbyterian, Washington, D.C.: Did I hear you say 1,500 businesses have left the District? What is being done to rebuild confidence in the business sector? And what is being done to boost minority business enterprise in the District of Columbia?

MAYOR BARRY: We have a small office of Business and Economic Development, which is trying to find out some of the problems facing businesses in the District and trying to create some incentives as opposed to disincentives.

For example, the printing industry was moving out of Washington into Maryland and Virginia. When we checked into it, we found that land cost was one reason, but another reason was that we treated printing presses as personal property for tax purposes while Maryland and Virginia did not. Therefore, we are going to amend our tax laws to make them at least competitive in that area.

We also found that a number of business people have difficulty getting through the licensing procedures. It takes forever to get a business license, and an occupancy license, and go to the Zoning Commission, and so forth. Now we are establishing a one-stop service center where businesses can get one license that can be multiplied through the other license bureaus without delay.

We are talking to people, trying to convince them that they ought to stay in the District, giving them a sense of confidence about the District. Again, it is not easy. We are helped somewhat by the sewer moratorium in Montgomery County which is next-door to the District in Maryland. Businesses cannot build and expand out there. Another neighbor, Prince George's County, has sewer capacity, but they cannot attract as many people as they would like, and we are taking advantage of the situation.

We have a booming downtown development west of 15th Street; from 15th Street to Georgetown office buildings are mushrooming, and there is no more land to build on. We are now trying to expand east of 15th Street to North Capitol Street, from Pennsylvania Avenue to New York Avenue.

We will get our Housing Finance Agency off the ground as soon as the Congress approves our charter amendment. The House passed it last year, but the Senate did not. That will give us some added leverage in the bond market to borrow money. The agency can either subsidize some of the interest, or they can lend it at a little more than they paid, which would be about 5½ percent, maybe 6½ or 6¾ on the bond market.

As for minority businesses, we have one of the strongest laws in the country, which requires the D.C. government to award to competent and qualified minorities at least 25 percent of all our contracts for construction, goods, and services. We have not done that very well in the past, and I am determined to do better. I think we are up to an average of about 20 percent now, though some agencies are way down, and some are way up. Courtland Cox, the director of the Minority Business Opportunity Commission is pushing hard to make sure that we do better. We are in touch with the Greater Washington Business

Center, people at the Small Business Administration, and with the Office of Minority Business Enterprise at the U.S. Department of Commerce to try to generate more minority-owned businesses and more businesses for people who happen to belong to a minority group.

ROBERT GOLDWIN, American Enterprise Institute: The question of unemployment and youth unemployment is a matter of tremendous importance in the city. One of the things I work on is the relation of education to unemployment.

People who know much more about statistics than I do say it is hard to be sure about unemployment and youth unemployment figures. But in all the Labor Department tables unemployment and years of education are always correlated. People with five years of education beyond high school consistently have one-fifth the unemployment rate of those who have not finished high school; differences of race or locality do not make much difference.

You may be right that some of the high school graduates this year will have trouble finding a job, especially at first. But it will be even tougher for those who do not finish high school, and it will stay tougher for the rest of their lives. On the other hand, those who get through college will have low unemployment figures that will continue and will get lower.

My question is really about education in the city. What can be done to upgrade the schools in the city and to improve the attitude of the children to persuade them of the vital importance of education to their lives?

MAYOR BARRY: We are limited in the District because the School Board has authority over the day-to-day instructional program and disbursements. I have no authority over that, except once a year when they submit their proposed budget to me and I either keep it the same, raise it, or lower it and send it to the Council.

But I am trying to create a different kind of atmosphere and attitude toward education. I have been talking to parents. One of the missing ingredients in the District is parental involvement. I am not concerned with the governance question—with whether the School Board should be appointed or elected—because we have to deal first with the whole question of parent and student involvement. For instance, during the teachers' strike, the parents should have been outraged. They should have come down to my office or the board's office, up in arms about it, and demanded to know what was going on. They did not, in any large number.

I am putting together a program to involve D.C. government

employees. I don't know how many of them have children in the public schools of the District, but I'm going to find out. I think I can involve them in a very direct way, but I'm not yet ready to announce this program.

In conclusion, let me say that the correlation of unemployment and education is also a fact of race. College graduates who are black are at the same unemployment level as high school graduates who are white. There are some other statistics, too, that say race is still a serious factor in employment in this country.